quantum healing and awareness

how to get access to the information level of reality

Foreword

Some years ago I was in a bad condition. I was not well both physically and mentally. With regard to my physical problems, orthodox medicine was able to dampen some of my physical symptoms, but ultimately the goal was less to heal me and more to prevent a further deterioration of my health. I had sought the advice of a therapist for my psychological problems. This also helped me to feel slightly better. But a success, a breakthrough, a real solution to my problems could not be achieved here either.

At this point I could have given up and accepted my fate. Yes, my health was not good. But there are people who are much worse off. And indeed, orthodox medicine had succeeded in permanently preventing   a further deterioration of my health condition with the appropriate medication. And yes, I was not well mentally either. But who is really happy? We all have our problems, right?

But since it is not in my nature to simply accept conditions that are not tenable for me without comment, I have turned to alternative healing methods. In the following 12 to 18 months I invested a lot of time and also a lot of money to try almost all common alternative healing methods. (The latter, however, only at the beginning, i.e. until I had enough experience to see through the charlatans at first sight. More about this later in this book). And as with orthodox medicine and also the classical psychological approaches in the form of talk therapy, I was able to perceive an alleviation of my suffering. The alternative healing methods really helped me, one more, the other less. But the big breakthrough, the success, the feeling of being in the state I was supposed to be in, both physically and psychologically, was still missing.

Finally a good friend of mine gave me a book about quantum healing. And I was skeptical at first, as you might be, and rightly so. After all, there are a lot of quacks, charlatans or unscrupulous businessmen, especially in the field of esotericism and alternative healing methods, who have no moral qualms about exploiting the real suffering and desperation of people with empty promises for their own financial interests. But I have - and maybe it was just for the sake of this good friend - dealt with the subject and finally just gave it a try. The book was free as a gift and the practice of quantum healing takes only a few minutes. So what harm can it do.

Well, what can I say: My very badly running insulin-dependent type 2 diabetes with sometimes several and also severe hypoglycemia per week has softened to the extent that today I only have to take a small tablet for breakfast and also pay less attention to my diet. My back pain has completely disappeared. I was able to solve my relationship problems, or rather, the good friend who gave me the book is now my wife, and the second child is on the way. By sheer coincidence, as I thought at the time, but possibly as a direct result of the quantum healing, as I suspect today, a new professional perspective has opened up for me. And, perhaps the most important thing for me: I have succeeded in overcoming my pride and reestablishing contact with my father after years of silence between us.

And all this within less than three months.

Due to my success, I have continued to practice quantum healing both for myself and for other people. Some of these people have also practiced quantum healing themselves and applied it to other people. Using this positive wave effect, which is actually a characteristic feature of the functional principle on which quantum healing is based, I would like to share my experiences with you in the form of this book. I will not limit myself to the pure technique of quantum healing, but will also give you information about the historical and scientific background. I will present the different possibilities, how and to which groups of people, as well as to which types of diseases quantum healing can be applied. I will give you a lot of tips and tricks how you can and should maintain your physical as well as mental health in order to avoid getting into a state of illness that requires quantum consciousness, another alternative healing method or conventional medicine. In essence, however, it will be about the information level of our reality mentioned in the title, on which not only quantum healing, but also many other alternative healing methods and partly even orthodox medicine are based.

At this point I would like to tell you a little joke: "There are three types of people. Those who can count to three, and those who can't." But joke aside, and it was not a particularly good one anyway; there are indeed three kinds of people. And before we get started, I would like to ask you to take a minute to find out what kind of person you are.

Option number one: You believe that alternative healing methods work and now you would like to learn about quantum healing. In this case, you should read this book because it will give you access to a subject area that you are not familiar with yet. Or perhaps you have already informed yourself about quantum healing, perhaps this is already the second or third book you are reading on this topic, or perhaps you are already actively practicing quantum healing and have acquired this book with the intention of continuing your education. In this case I recommend that you read this book as well, because the information level aspect is based on scientific knowledge that is so new that even in the world of quantum physics and quantum healing it is still unexplored territory.

Option number two: You are skeptical. Very good! Im likes skeptics, rather than people who just believe everything you tell them because it sounds good or confirms their own world view in a twisted way. And you are absolutely right to be skeptical, because, as already mentioned, there are a lot of black sheep in the world of alternative healing methods. I also consider myself a skeptic and a realist. But in my opinion, a critical mind like yours needs not only to critically examine a certain subject matter, but also to put your own skepticism and prejudices to the test again and again in order to give yourself the opportunity to allow a change of your own opinion and world view. So in this case too, from one skeptic to another, I recommend that you read this book. With pleasure also with wrinkled forehead. And perhaps I will not succeed in convincing you of the reality of quantum healing and the existence of the information level. But if nothing else, then you have informed yourself about a topic you were not familiar with before, and perhaps you will be able to filter out partial information at least in some places of this book that is interesting and relevant for you personally.

Option number three: You are a denier. You think this book is bullshit and I am a nutcase. All people who believe in alternative healing methods are in your eyes idiots on the spiritual level of naive children. And no matter what I write here, no matter what arguments I bring, I will not be able to change your opinion. Because you are simply right. And that's because you are, period. In this case, I would actually ask you to stop reading this line now. Not only because you are wasting your valuable time, but especially because I have put a lot of effort into this book and I am simply worth more to myself than to be laughed at by a narrow-minded concrete head.

Now that this has been cleared up, I hope you enjoy reading.

The basics of quantum healing

The historical background

The concept of quantum healing and the quantum consciousness associated with it, or rather the technique of quantum healing, was first coined by the American Deepak Chopra in the 1980s. As a famous author of books on spirituality and alternative medicine, which are not only respected in esoteric circles, Chopra was the first to establish a connection between the effectiveness of alternative healing methods and the scientifically recognized laws of quantum physics. Based on the double-slit experiment conducted by the physicist Thomas Young as early as 1902, which scientifically proved that the movement of particles on the atomic level of our reality is not only influenced by an observer, i.e. by consciousness, but can even take the course that the observer consciously expects, he developed the theory of "Quantum Healing", which can be understood as the basis of modern quantum healing practiced today.

Disseminated in books and lectures, Chopra's derivation quickly gained great attention and triggered a public discussion about the possibility or impossibility of the theories he developed, until finally the American chiropractor Frank Kinslow put the theory of Quantum Healing on a concrete and applicable basis at the end of the 1980s with the technique of Quantum Entrainment, which he developed. As a chiropractor and luminary in the field of Transcendental Meditation, Kinslow dedicated his life to the study of body and soul, with a focus on the creative intelligence of human beings. The Quantum Entrainment technique he developed can be seen as the crowning achievement of his life's work. More information about the Quantum Entrainment technique will be available later in this book in a chapter dedicated to this topic.

Almost simultaneously, and based on the same theories of quantum physics and quantum consciousness, Dr. Richard Bartlett developed his technique of Matrix Energetics, with which he added a physical component to the principle of healing through pure consciousness developed by Kinslow for the targeted manipulation of body-internal energy flows and quantum waves. In the further course of this book, a separate chapter will also be dedicated to his techniques and findings.

From about 2009 onwards, the theories and techniques of quantum healing gained worldwide attention. In the meantime, even in rather conservative Germany, the theory of quantum healing has become a widely applied reality as an alternative or support to conventional medical procedures, as well as the subject of scientific studies and discussions.

There may be differences of opinion as to whether it makes sense to speak of a *history of quantum healing* in a new method that was only developed in the 1980s and has only been in use and receiving worldwide attention for just over ten years. It is undisputed, however, that the techniques of quantum healing and quantum consciousness have existed and been successfully practiced for thousands of years. These techniques, which will be discussed in more detail later in this book, can be clearly associated with a variety of healing methods that were already used in ancient Egypt, Taoism and by the Hawaiian shamans called Kahunas. The basic principle and the confirmed mode of action of quantum healing is therefore by no means new.

The concepts of quantum healing, quantum consciousness and quantum physics merely provide an explanatory model for a healing method that has been successfully practiced for thousands of years.

The scientific background

The basic principle of quantum healing as well as the successfully practiced techniques based on this basic principle are based on the scientific fact of the existence of a quantum level of our reality, which is researched within the framework of the likewise recognized and fact-based quantum physics and is already being implemented in the most modern technology. But what exactly is quantum physics? And how is it possible that behind the reality we perceive every day of our lives there is a second reality in the form of a quantum level on which completely different laws of nature prevail? It is difficult for people who have not intensively studied this topic to understand quantum physics. And it is also difficult to understand quantum physics for people who have dealt with this topic very intensively due to personal interest or even as part of a physics degree. However, the laws that govern our reality at the quantum level elude all logic and in many cases even radically contradict what we humans generally regard as common *sense.*

An example: A soccer player slips on the penalty kick. The ball then moves on a track that takes it far past the goal. Now the soccer player looks at the flying ball in a very concentrated and conscious manner and wishes that the ball lands in the goal, whereupon the ball actually changes its direction of flight, passes the goalkeeper and bulges the net in the middle of the goal. Completely impossible, you will think now, and you are of course completely right about the level of reality you perceive as reality, on which we all are and interact. On the quantum level, on the other hand, this is not only absolutely possible, but has even been proven beyond doubt by the aforementioned double-slit experiment by Thomas Young in 1902.

A second example: You invent a time machine and travel back in time to kill Hitler. But if you killed Hitler in the past, he never existed in the present, and you would have had no reason to invent a time machine and travel back in time. This very well known example based on the logical problem of cause and effect is often used as an argument why time travel is not possible. But on the quantum level of our reality the law of cause and effect has no validity. In quantum physics it is absolutely normal, for example, that effect occurs first and then cause, or that an effect occurs without a cause, or that these two factors exist completely independently of each other, or that, to top it all off, an effect in the present is an effect one million light years away to a cause and causes a thousand years in the past. Albert Einstein already said that there are no physical laws that would prohibit the possibility of time travel. Quantum physics offers the explanation why the man was right with this statement, just as it also provides the explanatory model for why healing methods that have been successfully practiced for thousands of years work.

A third example: In a small town there is exactly one hairdresser. This hairdresser, and here the exact formulation is important, cuts the hair of all people who do not cut their own hair. So who cuts the hair of the hairdresser?

1. He could cut his own hair. But then he cuts his own hair and by definition he cannot cut his own hair, because he does not cut the hair of people who cut their own hair.

2. Maybe his wife cuts his hair. But in that case he does not cut his own hair and therefore cuts his own hair, because he cuts the hair of all people who do not cut their own hair.

3. Maybe he just lets his hair grow. But even in this case he does not cut his own hair, and by definition cuts his own hair with it.

This is a classic example of an either/or, yes/no decision. On the level of reality that we perceive as reality, black cannot be white and white cannot be black and yes cannot be no and no cannot be yes. On the quantum level this is not a problem at all. Schrödinger's cat is simultaneously dead and alive on the quantum level until someone on our reality level opens the lid and thus forces a decision.

This may all seem very complicated, but actually it is not. To understand quantum physics, at least in its fundamentals, it is sufficient to accept it. Accept the fact that there are physical laws that cannot be explained with common sense. Accept the fact that below the reality you perceive as reality there is another level of reality which has about the same function for our reality as the foundation of a house for the first floor, the second floor and the roof. Accept the fact that the capacity, the intellectual capacity of your mind is limited. The word "mind" comes from "understand". There are things that your mind cannot understand. But the human psyche consists not only of mind, but also of consciousness. Use your consciousness to simply accept the physically and mathematically provable reality of the quantum plane and the physical laws that apply to it.

What does all this have to do with quantum healing? Quite simply. On the quantum level it is possible that a cat is dead and alive at the same time, that cause and effect exist independently of each other, and that a physical object, such as an atom, changes its direction of movement due to observation, i.e. due to *consciousness.* And from this now three conclusions can be deduced, both in the form of common sense and in the form of a scientifically tenable logical chain of arguments.

1. At the quantum level, a person is both healthy and sick at the same time. On the reality level, which we perceive as reality, a person is *either* healthy *or* he is sick. There is no other possibility. On the quantum level, however, he exists in both states simultaneously, just as Schrödinger's cat is dead and alive at the same time. If a person is now ill, then this solid state exists only on our level of reality. On the quantum level, he is still both at the same time. Quantum healing offers us the possibility, to take a somewhat bizarre example, to put the human being back into his own individual box and close the lid, whereupon the human being again exists in both states simultaneously, sick and healthy. And when we open the lid again, thus forcing one of the two states as an integral part of our reality, we *consciously choose* to bring about the state of being healthy in our either/or decision.

2. At the quantum level, cause and effect are interchangeable and/or can interact independently of each other in space and time. If a person is first

healthy and then becomes ill, there is a reason for it, a cause. In addition, there is a very concrete point in time when the human body changes from a state of health to a state of illness, just as when you throw a stone into a lake and create waves, there is also a very concrete point in time when the cause changes into the effect. With quantum healing we can create an effect through our consciousness as the cause at a point in time when the person was not yet ill. So we can change the possibility state from sick to healthy back to a point in time *before* the possibility state has changed from healthy to sick at all. In relation to our reality defined by space and time, this would result in the situation that we do not heal an illness, but make sure that it has never existed. This would have given us no reason to heal this illness in the present, but as already mentioned, this is not a problem on the quantum level.

3. At the quantum level it is possible not only to change the direction of motion of a physical particle, such as an atom, through consciousness and observation, but even to redirect it in the direction desired by the observer. If this works with one particle, it also works with two. Or with two thousand. Or with two million. Or with two trillions. And then we can also change the behavior of objects made of these particles, such as a human body, through our consciousness. Of course, there are limits here. But with quantum healing, we can at least influence the behavior of these particles, as well as the

behavior of all particles connected to them at the quantum level, to such an extent that diseases can be cured, money worries solved or unfulfilled professional or relationship wishes realized.

So you can see that the basics of quantum healing can be explained and understood on a scientific level with a little common sense and logical thinking, as long as you really let yourself be guided by logic instead of prejudices. If science says that one plus one equals two, if physics and mathematics say that one plus one equals two, if the real experiences of hundreds of thousands and millions of people can only be explained by the fact that one plus one equals two, and if there is then a small group of people who simply do not want to believe this because they cannot imagine it, then the mistake is not in science. There are also people who deny climate change, corona or even the fact that the earth is a sphere, no matter how much evidence and scientific facts there may be.

From pseudo-science to conventional medicine

Some people or groups of people like to call quantum healing a pseudoscience, simply ignoring the quantitatively measurable successes of hundreds of thousands of people. At this point I will not bother to convince or try to defend the measurable and explainable reality of quantum healing with sound arguments. I provided an explanation in the previous chapter, and whoever wants to make a decision of belief or disbelief absolutely and with all power and force under exclusion of any logical thinking about this factual subject, does so because of a personal motivation, which has nothing to do with this book or this subject. In short: My time is simply too precious for me to have a discussion with people who, when you run out of arguments, become personally offensive or criticize spelling mistakes.

What I would like to do, however, is to take a closer look at the concept of pseudoscience. I believe that before discussing a matter, one should first be clear about what exactly one is discussing, instead of bombarding the discussion partner with buzzwords and hollow phrases in the traditional populist manner.

The exact definition of the word "pseudoscience" is as follows:

> Pseudoscience is a term for claims, teachings, theories, practices and institutions that claim to be scientific or are apparently scientific but do not meet the requirements of scientificity, **especially the criterion of verifiability.**

Pseudoscience is thus defined as a theory, a fact or a certain applied practice and methodology, the effects of which may have been proven and documented, but cannot be **proven beyond doubt**, i.e. verified, with common scientific methods. This applies, among other things, to any form of psychotherapy and psychoanalysis, to - and I emphasize this explicitly - **anthropogenic** climate change, as well as to not all, but nevertheless wide areas of quantum physics and quantum mechanics, which, although existing only in the non-verifiable theory, are then again recognized in scientific circles and accepted as reality.

There was a time when it was considered a consensus that the earth is a disk. People who claimed otherwise could get into serious trouble with this and perhaps even, in extreme cases, face imprisonment or even death penalty in the form of a funeral pyre. Rightly so, some scientists would now claim, who have dedicated their lives to the ardent fight against pseudo-science. In that dark period of our history, the claim that the earth is a sphere was not verifiable due to the lack of scientific technology.

At another time, not quite so far in the past, but before scientific technology was mature enough to allow the construction of microscopes, some doctors postulated the existence of organisms invisible to the naked eye and claimed that these microorganisms, called *bacteria,* were responsible for many diseases and infections. Their demand that, for example, surgeons should wash their hands before surgery was met with ridicule and incomprehension, and in some cases even with exclusion from the medical community.

When I was born, computers were still as big as trucks. Instead of microchips they were powered by tubes. And information was not stored on hard disks, CDs or floppy disks, but on punched cards, i.e. on cardboard discs into which holes were punched. Even back then, there were people who claimed that one day, perhaps in a few hundred or thousand years, there would be a computer in every household. Society in general and science in particular dubbed these people as a bunch of aloof freaks. Not even the imagination of these crackpots was enough to imagine that one day every person would carry a palm-sized computer with an integrated transceiver in his or her trouser pocket, the performance of which would exceed that of those first computers by a factor of billions.

Acupuncture was long considered a pseudo-science. Today it is offered by many general practitioners as an alternative treatment or as a support to conventional medical treatment. The costs for this are covered by health insurance.

Homeopathy was and is still partly called pseudo-science, although more and more health insurance companies are covering the costs of this alternative medical treatment. And I think one can assume that there are no gullible nutcases on the boards of health insurance companies.

This could go on forever now. In fact, it would be possible to fill an entire book on the subject, with countless verifiable examples from human history, starting from the time when a Stone Age man first had the idea of banging two stones against each other to see if there might be a spark. But as I said, it is not the aim of this book to convince people who have imprisoned their only seemingly critical spirit in a pseudo-intellectual ivory tower of scientific ignorance. Quantum healing is a factual reality whose effects have been proven ten thousand times and a hundred thousand times. The absence of scientific technology, with which the effects of quantum healing cannot be proven and made physically visible, at least for the moment, will not change this truth.

The information level

In the previous chapters you were told *that* quantum healing works. In addition, you were explained *how* quantum healing works, i.e. which scientific and quantum physical laws form the basis of the explainable mode of action of quantum healing. But as promised in the foreword, the core topic of this book is not about that or how quantum healing works, but why.

In order to explain the why in a comprehensible way, some bows have to be struck at this point.

You have learned that, simply put, there are basically two realities. One is our reality experienced as daily reality, consisting of a three-dimensional space that moves forward through time in a straight line. In this space there are objects ranging from the size of planets and galaxies to molecules and atomic and subatomic particles, which are in constant motion and incessantly interact with each other, i.e. influence each other and are in constant interaction.

The other reality is the quantum level, where particles even smaller than atomic or subatomic particles, the so-called quarks and strings, move on a level where the classical concept of space and time no longer exists and the laws of nature, which we perceive as immutable, are suspended. But no matter how radically different our *normal* reality and quantum reality may be from each other, they are similar in one respect: on both levels of reality there are moving particles that interact with each other. For in this way, and *only in* this way, through moving particles of whatever size, which influence each other through their motion, it is possible for our reality and quantum reality to interact with each other, which is the basic prerequisite for quantum healing to work.

For the next step on the way to explaining *why* quantum healing works, we need to leave the quantum plane for a moment and take a closer look at our three-dimensional space-time universe.

Already Albert Einstein proved scientifically with his theory of relativity that there is a connection between space and time. Or, more precisely, that there is a connection between speed and time. You have certainly heard that time passes more slowly for an object that moves very fast than for an object that moves very slowly or not at all. And the faster an object moves through space, the slower it moves through time, until, purely theoretically, when it reaches the speed of light, time comes to a complete standstill.

The nearest planet in our neighborhood is about four light-years away. If we were to build a spaceship that moves   at 97% of the speed of light, then from our perspective, i.e. from Earth, this spaceship would take four years to reach its destination. But for a pilot who is inside this spaceship, only about two days would pass, because the energy necessary for a steady flow of time is subtracted from time and converted into speed. If the spaceship were to move at 98% of the speed of light, then from our perspective it would also take about four years to reach its destination. For the pilot, however, only seven minutes would pass at this distance and at this speed. At a speed approaching that of light at 99%, it would still take four years when viewed from the outside, but for the pilot it would take only a few microseconds, too little time to even

23

consciously perceive its passage. And if we were to succeed, which is unfortunately completely impossible physically, in building a spaceship that actually moves at 100% of the speed of light, then the travel time perceived from the outside would still be four years. However, the time that passes for the pilot would then be exactly zero in this case. So there is no microsecond, no millionth microsecond or billionth microsecond, but simply zero. For the pilot, exactly zero time would pass.

In this one single frozen moment all movement ends. The pilot no longer moves. The cells in his body no longer work. The molecules that make up his cells no longer move. The movements on the atomic level, that is, the movement of protons and neutrons and the electrons orbiting them cease to exist. And even down to the quantum level, where only quarks and strings interact with each other, the motionlessness continues. Complete, absolute standstill of all particles, no matter what size or level of reality.

This is exactly the state that science is trying to bring about by experimenting in the particle accelerator.

You know the principle of the particle accelerator. In a magnetic tube kilometers long, tiny particles are accelerated to a speed as close as possible to the speed of light. Probably the best known device of its kind is located at the CERN Institute in Switzerland and is considered a pioneer in the discovery of groundbreaking scientific principles.

The basic principle of this approach is actually relatively simple. A particle, as already mentioned, is accelerated to the speed of light, i.e. it is brought into that state in which time ceases to exist. For this particle, but only for this particle, for a period of time that, when viewed from the outside, lasts only a few milliseconds, all motion stops at the atomic and subatomic level as well as at the quantum level. For the scientists conducting this experiment, however, time continues to run in normal orbits, allowing them to observe a particle that is completely in a state of timelessness and motionlessness and to derive scientific knowledge from this observation.

In November 2019, very recently, a breakthrough has been made, a scientific discovery that has the potential to redefine our understanding of our universe and the quantum universe. The observation of particles in the state of the speed of light, i.e. in the state of timelessness and motionlessness, and the presentation of the scientific data obtained from this observation in the form of a highly complex mathematical formula has led to the existence of a further level of reality, the so-called **information level, which has** not yet been fully proven, but which is urgently suspected.

Remember: Our normal plane of reality consists of moving particles that are in constant interaction with each other, following the rules of natural laws. The quantum level, which is below our normal level of reality, also consists of moving particles that are in constant interaction with each other, following the rules of natural laws that apply at the quantum level. At the newly discovered **information level**, which is located below the quantum level, the agreement between all levels of our reality is no longer valid. At the information level there are no more particles. On the information level there are also no more laws of nature. All that still exists on the information level is pure, pure information itself.

This sounds very adventurous in the first moment, but is actually very easy to explain and logical to understand.

Imagine you are playing a computer game on your computer. For example a flight simulator. Since this computer game should be as realistic as possible, laws of nature such as aerodynamics or gravity are also simulated, because otherwise the game would not make sense. This computer game, this picture that you see on your screen, in which a moving particle, namely the time of flight, follows certain laws of nature that apply on our level of reality, is the world in which you live.

But where does this picture come from? What is the reason why the plane changes its direction of movement when you press a button? Exactly. From a computer program, namely the game you play. And this game, this computer program consists of a computer code. This code is made up of tens of thousands or even hundreds of thousands of pages of text described with letters, numbers and special characters. This computer code, which in this example represents the quantum level, has nothing, but also nothing at all to do with the image on your screen. It is simply text, nothing else. And yet this text is the reason why an airplane consisting of shapes and colors moves within certain simulated laws of nature on your screen.

But where does this text come from? Where is the cause for this computer program? Exactly. On your hard disk!

The cause of the moving image on your computer screen is a program written in computer code. And this program is stored as information on your hard disk. And that is all that is stored on your hard disk. Information. The processes that process this information and eventually transform it into a moving image on your screen are performed in other components of your computer. Your hard disk only contains the information necessary for these processes.

And it contains *all* information. Your computer games, your movies, your music, your pictures. The programs you work with, such as text programs or Excel. The operating system without which your computer could not function. All this is stored as information on your hard drive. But beyond the information itself, your hard drive contains nothing. And if you don't remove or add data, nothing on your hard drive changes. Nothing *happens* there! Nothing moves. You could remove the hard drive from your computer, put it in a drawer for ten years, and when you take it out, the hard drive still contains exactly the same information as it did ten years ago. Nothing changes or moves on your hard drive. It is simply a storage for pure, pure information.

It is exactly the same with the information level of our reality. Schrödinger's cat is dead and alive at the same time, because the information for both states is stored on the information level. At the quantum level, the cat *exists* in both states, in the form of an object that is subject to the laws of nature at the quantum level. On our reality level, the cat *exists* in *one of* these states, and again as an object that is subject to the laws of nature on our reality level. But on the information level, this cat does not exist, nor any laws of nature to which it could be subject. Everything that exists is the pure, pure information, which is stored unchangeably and for all times as a possible blueprint for the cat in all only imaginable states.

Why does quantum healing work? You press a key on your keyboard and the simulated plane on your computer screen moves to the left. At that moment, your computer accesses the part of the computer code stored on your hard drive that contains the information for movement. This information includes both left and right movement. But you only realize one of them.

They are sick. On the information level, the information for your state of health is stored. This information contains both your sick and your healthy state. With your consciousness you first call up this information, then you realize this information in the form of moving particles on the quantum level, where they exist in physical form in both states at the same time and then, also through your consciousness, force in our reality an also physical form in one of the two states, namely healthy.

This is the reason why quantum healing works. The existence of an information level still existing below the quantum level is the reason why quantum healing works and is practiced successfully by hundreds of thousands of people on a regular basis. In addition, the existence of the information level is also the reason why many other alternative healing methods work, such as visualization or homeopathy, which will be discussed in more detail later in this book.

But now enough of theorizing! Now that I have explained to you in detail and plausibly and comprehensibly how and why quantum healing works, I don't want to keep you in suspense any longer. In the next chapter I will now present the different techniques that you can try out immediately without any further delay and without any practice.

The techniques of quantum heal-ing

The Quantum Entrainment Method by Frank Kinslow

A s the founder of quantum healing, the Quantum Entrainment technique developed by Frank Kinslow is honored to be mentioned first in this chapter. It is probably the fastest and most direct way to access the state of being healthy stored at the information level. Working with a certified quantum healer is as unnecessary as experience. You can simply try it out yourself. All alone and without you having ever dealt with the subject before. You don't have to worry, it is basically impossible in quantum healing to inflict harm on yourself or others unintentionally through a wrong application of the techniques. There is a reason for this, but at this point it would go beyond the scope of this article. To give preference to a simple explanation: Just imagine that your hard disk has copy protection or that the administrator (the really big one. You know who I mean.) has not given you the authorization to make changes on the information level. So just try it, you can't break anything.

Through the technique of Quantum Entrainment, you can put your mind, soul and body into a state of calm and relaxation within seconds by taking a conscious inner step. The core element in this method is pure, unadulterated consciousness, which gives you access to the pure, unadulterated data sets of the information level. The founder of this technique, Frank Kinslow, calls this pure consciousness *Awareness*. In the further course of this book you will encounter this term more often.

But how exactly does this method work?

Quite simply, you put yourself in the role of the observer. You do not try hard, you do not evaluate, you do not concentrate. All you do is observe. And if you do it wrong, if you do make an effort, then you observe your effort. If you do evaluate, then observe your evaluation. If you approach it with a certain expectation, then observe your expectation. Do not try to put your thoughts to rest. Observe them. Do not try to suppress unpleasant emotions or ignore physical discomfort. If you suffer, then observe your suffering. If you are in pain, then observe your pain. All these factors are the moving particles of our level of reality, subject to the laws of nature. By not trying to change anything, you bring yourself, so to speak, to the same frequency on which the unchanging information level exists and within a few seconds you receive, in a single step, the data necessary for your recovery.

And that was it. And if you now think that this sounds too simple to work, then give it a try. You will find that the implementation is even easier and faster than the explanation.

In the realization of pure awareness, you will very quickly, within seconds, experience a feeling of peace and bliss, combined with an inner silence that cannot exist in our noisy and hectic universe with all its swirling particles and elements. This is the silence and timelessness of the unchanging level of information that you have access to at that exact moment. Most likely you will also experience a feeling of joy and well-being almost bordering on spirituality. This is commonly referred to as the central element of Quantum Entrainment and marks the moment in which, without any conscious action on your part, the state data of the information level on the quantum level are first brought to a physical existence and then transferred in the way you wish to the either/or state of our reality, resulting in an immediate improvement of your state.

This process can be a bit overwhelming, especially the first time. After all, billions of molecular, atomic and subatomic particles of your body are caused to change their direction of movement when you reformat. Don't worry if you feel a brief dizziness or, if you try this technique while standing, your body bends or swings. This is completely normal and will pass quickly.

This method is particularly recommended for emotional problems such as anxiety, depression, trauma, mood swings or obsessive-compulsive disorders. But even in the case of a physical illness, this technique will give you, if not complete healing, then at least a clearly noticeable and almost immediate relief.

The two-point, or Matrix Energetics method of Richard Bartlett

The two-point method was developed almost simultaneously with the Quantum Entrainment method by the American doctor Richard Bartlett. As with the Quantum Entrainment method, the core element of the Two-Point Method consists of pure consciousness, which gives the user of Quantum Healing access to the information level. In contrast, or more precisely as an extension or alternative to the Quantum Entrainment method, Bartlett's Two-Point Method incorporates a physical component into its mode of action. Thus, an actual physical contact is created at, as the name suggests, two points of the human body. This contact is usually performed by a quantum healer on a patient. But it is also possible to perform the two-point method on oneself.

A further difference can be derived from the naming of Bartlett's healing approach. It is not for nothing that the two-point method is also known as the Matrix Energetics method in those circles where quantum healing is successfully applied.

But what exactly is a matrix? And what does it have to do with quantum healing, and especially with the information level at the base of our reality?

In quantum medicine, the matrix is often referred to as the basis of reality, i.e. the ground on which our reality is built. Other descriptions, which are not false, but merely take a different perspective approach to describe the exact same thing, in other words, experience the matrix as an energy field interacting with other energy fields. In classical quantum physics, i.e. in that scientific field which, at least for the sake of appearance, exists independently of quantum healing, the matrix is referred to in corresponding physics textbooks as a zero point field and describes a space filled with pure information. Although there may sometimes be disagreements between classical physicists and quantum healers, it is undisputed and, despite differing world views, a common consensus that not only every living creature, but also every object of any size, from a galaxy, planet, stone, and even a molecule or atom, has a matrix, i.e. an energy field that interacts with all other energy fields on the energetic level as well as with all material particles on the physical level.

But be careful! Based on this description, do not fall into the assumption that the zero point field mentioned, i.e. this space filled with pure information, is the information plane. And by no means should the matrix as an energy field surrounding all physical objects be confused with the aura known from esotericism, which definitely exists and can also be perceived with classical scientific measuring methods, but is not part of this book and has nothing to do with the functioning of quantum healing. There is also aura healing as an alternative healing method, but in this case the information level is the explanation for the functioning of aura healing, and not the other way around. You will learn more about this later in this book.

No, the matrix is an energy field surrounding all material particles, which propagates in the form of a static wave from the material object in its center in all directions up to theoretical infinity and thus anchors the said central and physical particle object in reality. As I said, these are not my words or those of quantum healers, but those of classical quantum physicists, who unfortunately in many cases consider quantum healing to be humbug, simply ignoring the clearly visible similarities.

What exactly does this mean for quantum healing? As in most cases, this is again explained very simply in principle. You have experienced that you exist in the state of being sick *or* in the state of being healthy in the macro-universe, that is, on our normal level of reality. You have realized that you exist in the state of being sick *and in the state of being* healthy on the quantum level. You now know that the information for these two states is stored as a non-existent theoretical possibility on the information level and can be brought into physical existence by you through pure consciousness on the quantum level and finally be realized on the macro level through a conscious decision.

But how is it actually possible that your consciousness gives you access to the information level?

The answer is as simple as it is predictable: Through your matrix.

The matrix is a static energy field that extends from you in all directions to the theoretical infinity. And with *all* directions *all* directions are actually meant. So not only the spatial directions on our macro level, but also all directions on the quantum and information level. It is your matrix that connects you to the macro level, i.e. our *normal* universe, as well as to the quantum level and the information level, and it is this matrix that makes it possible for you to be present on all levels, even if in completely different states. And it is precisely this connection that enables you to access the level of pure information through pure consciousness, in order to retrieve the data for the state of health you desire.

As complicated as this explanation may seem, the implementation of the two-point method is simple. The quantum healer places two fingers on different parts of the patient's body and puts himself in the state of pure consciousness. In this way he accesses the information level and retrieves the data he wants. But what may sound very simple here is radical at the quantum level. For what the healer actually achieves by touching the patient's body at two points in the state of pure consciousness and accessing the information level via the matrix as a catalyst is that, very simply put, he causes a short circuit in the matrix. For the least imaginable amount of time, he causes the patient's energy field to collapse. And when it is restored at almost the same moment, the information in this energy field, which previously defined the patient's condition as *sick*, is overwritten with the records from the information level defined as *healthy.*

You do not need to worry. As mentioned before, it is not possible to do harm   with quantum healing. But be aware that this approach is radical, albeit at the quantum level. Your matrix is switched off for a fraction of a millisecond and restarted with altered information. This can lead to you being hit by an inner wave of energy. Although not unpleasant, on the contrary, patients find it extremely pleasant and relaxing in practically all cases, it regularly happens that patients lose their balance and fall backwards during treatments that are performed while standing. Therefore, if you use the two-point method in this way, you should take appropriate safety precautions and either place a sofa or soft mat behind you, or ask a person you trust to catch you in an emergency.

Of course you can also practice the two-point method while lying down. In addition, as already mentioned, it is not absolutely necessary to have this method performed by an experienced healer. You can also practice this method yourself, just like the Quantum Entrainment method, without experience and right now. However, if you want to do this on your own, I strongly advise you to try this method lying down first.

There is another significant difference between the Quantum Entrainment method and the two-point method. In the Quantum Entrainment method you put yourself in the role of a pure observer. You have no expectation. In the Two-Point Method, however, it is not only possible to perform the healing with a specific intention, but in fact the intention, i.e. the expectation, is the core element of the methodology introduced by Richard Bartlett.

Of course, a specific intention is not absolutely necessary. In most cases this method is performed by a healer. You may not want to tell him or her intimate details of your illness or personal problems, such as relationship problems and money worries. But if there is a relationship of trust between you and your healer, or if you are simply using this method on yourself, it is beneficial to do the procedure with a specific goal in mind.

At the information level, information is stored for your entire life in all imaginable states. If you want to watch a movie that is stored on your computer's hard drive, you need to navigate through your folder structure to place the arrow key of your mouse exactly where the movie is. The two-point method is similar. The more precisely you define the information you want to retrieve on the information level, e.g. a physical illness, relationship problems, money worries, an unfulfilled career wish, the more clearly the new information can be written into your restructured matrix.

But as I said, this is an advantage, but not absolutely necessary. Especially in the beginning you may have inhibitions about sharing intimate details of your life or physical illness with an experienced quantum healer you may have contacted only recently. In that case, simply let yourself be healed on a general, all-encompassing basis. Who knows; if you improve your overall state of life, rather than focusing on a single issue, doors may open that you never even thought existed before.

The Matrix Awareness Method after Roland Rocher and Rosi Lutz

With the introduction of Matrix Awareness, also known as the Three-Point Method, we are now leaving the United States, where the founding fathers of quantum healing originally made their new concept based on modern scientific knowledge available to a broad global public, and are moving to Switzerland. So you can see how quickly this new methodology has also become established in the international arena and has attracted a great deal of attention. It was a collaboration between the two Swiss Roland Rocher and Rosi Lutz, who after intensive research in the field of quantum theory and years of successful practice and experimentation with quantum healing, were able to achieve a breakthrough in the application of the said techniques. Whereby the word *was*, i.e. past tense, cannot be used adequately here, since the method of Matrix Awareness is adapted and optimized in a continuous process to the latest scientific methods and findings.

The Matrix Awareness Method is also called the Three-Point Method because it is a combination of the Two-Point Method and the Quantum Entrainment Method and combines the best of two similar healing methods. In Quantum Entrainment, when the user puts himself in the state of pure consciousness in order to gain access to the information level of reality, it is when the Two-Point Method is applied by an experienced healer, the healer himself, who puts himself in the state of pure consciousness when touching the patient with two fingers. In this case, the intervention of the patient is no longer necessary.

The Matrix Awareness Method combines only these two factors, and enhances them by adding another element.

A healer touches the patient at two points of his body and thereby puts himself in the state of pure consciousness. The patient himself also puts himself into the state of pure consciousness. The resulting unified *energy of consciousness* is not summed up, but rather potentiated, thus growing in its unified power to more than just the sum of its parts. In this state of exaggerated clarity and extreme connectedness to the information level, the healer now suggests spoken images to the patient. There is thus a transfer between the unanticipated technique of Quantum Entrainment and the conscious intention based technique of Matrix Energetics.

The suggestions should be as concrete as possible. So instead of "You will get better physically", a concrete "Your lower back pain will disappear" should be chosen. And instead of "Your living conditions will improve", rather a "Your financial problems will be solved by a new professional opportunity for you". Remember that the information for all possible states is stored on the information level. The more detailed you define the data you want, the easier it will be for you and the healer to access the exact location on the information level where the desired data for your healing is stored.

The method of Matrix Awareness invented by Roland Rocher and Rosi Lutz, through the combination of two tried and tested techniques that have been successfully performed tens of thousands of times, represents perhaps the most powerful tool in quantum physics and quantum healing based on it. But unfortunately there are also two disadvantages.

The first disadvantage is that for understandable reasons this technique cannot be performed alone. A collaboration with an experienced healer or a person of your trust, who is also experienced in the techniques of quantum healing or at least interested enough to try it once, is indispensable.

The second disadvantage is that in contrast to the technique of Quantum Entrainment, which can be performed without expectation, and the ideally intentional technique of Matrix Energetics, which can also be performed without such a technique, in Matrix Awareness the intentional intention is not only the basic requirement, but the patient must also communicate it as concretely as possible to the healer, so that he can transfer the corresponding suggestions into the consciousness of the patient in the state of combined pure consciousness. For this reason the method of Matrix Awareness is not necessarily suitable for beginners. An intimate relationship of trust between the healer and the person to be healed is to be regarded as obligatory in this technique.

The original matrix method of the alternative practitioner Stephan Bratzel

The healing method developed by the alternative practitioner Stephan Bratzel with the help of the original matrix is actually not an independent technique of quantum healing and shall only be mentioned here for the sake of completeness.

Bratzel originally worked as a spiritual healer and, in his work as a recognized alternative practitioner, he also brought elements of energetic healing into his techniques. Among other things, it was he who recognized that the method of quantum healing is by no means new, but has been practiced by advanced civilizations throughout human history. A clear correspondence between the aforementioned original healing methods and the technique of quantum healing became clear to him when he studied the elements of the Hawaiian Huna doctrine more closely in his work as a healer and energetic healer.

This technique is based on the idea that something like an original matrix exists. In other words, practically a blueprint for all forms of life that precisely defines the ideal state of every living being. This blueprint already exists before a human being is born and determines a considerable part of the path he will take during his life. In this concept, illness is defined as a faulty deviation from the path that has already been determined for us before we are born and is actually perfect. And through access to our original matrix, in the form of a spiritual intention, namely pure consciousness in combination with the techniques already described, access can be gained to the blueprint originally intended for us and the body, as well as the soul, can be returned to its natural state.

The application of the Ur-Matrix method does not differ essentially from the techniques already described. As said before, this technique shall be mentioned here only for the sake of completeness. However, it can be considered as fascinating that the original matrix method of Stephan Bratzel proved that quantum healing and its successful application is not a construct of our modern times. Even if the special techniques, with which quantum healing is practiced today, can perhaps be used more purposefully due to modern scientific knowledge and procedures, quantum healing as a basic concept and as an applied healing method has existed as long as the written history of mankind goes back into the past. In the end, modern science offers only a concrete explanation for a phenomenon that has existed for thousands of years.

The Timeline Method by Tad James and Wyatt Woodsmall

With the Timeline Method we go back to the America of the 80s, i.e. to the beginnings of quantum healing. It was the hypnosis specialist Tad James and the NLP trainer Wyatt Woodsmall who extended the then still novel concept of quantum healing by the technique of the Timeline method. In contrast to the techniques presented so far, this method should not be performed by beginners. A basic experience with the two-point method, which was described in detail in a previous chapter, is advisable here.

Like most of the techniques described so far, the Timeline method can be executed alone. However, as with the two-point method, it is recommended to perform this technique together with a trusted person or an experienced healer.

Another difference to the techniques presented so far is that the Timeline method is preferred for the correction of mental illness. A cure for physical problems is of course also possible, if only because many of the disorders in our matrix that manifest themselves on the physical plane are in fact manifestations of mental problems, or, as in the case of chronic tension pain, are the result of longstanding tension or incorrect postures that are also based on emotional problems.

As the name suggests, the Timeline method extends quantum healing by the factor of time. This means that the starting point of this technique is in our three-dimensional macro-universe, since the concept of time does not exist on the quantum level and the information level. But what does exist on these deeper layers of our reality is the information about what our physical and mental state looked like at a certain point in time on the level of our reality subject to the ancient laws of nature. It is exactly this data that we search for and find with the help of the Timeline method and then reintegrate into our matrix.

The implementation of the Timeline method is very simple, just like everything in quantum healing. The healer touches the patient in the same way as described in the chapter about the two-point method. Now the healer asks the patient about his age. After the healer has put himself in the state of pure consciousness, he slowly counts backwards   from the mentioned age in one-year steps. Firmly anchored in pure consciousness, the healer thus glides along the information assigned to the factor *time*, which is stored on the information level and still exists in a real existing state of possibility on the quantum level, where time does not exist.

This is, and you may allow me this personal remark, for me one of the most fascinating aspects of quantum healing, which makes the Timeline method for me the most fascinating technique of this form of alternative healing practice. In our macrocosm with its unchanging laws, nothing else happens but that the healer who is in the state of pure consciousness slowly counts backwards. On the quantum level, however, on which we *exist* simultaneously   in   all imaginable states at all times, we glide along the individual states that we have experienced and passed through in the course of our lives. So here, on a *physically real existing* level, a *real* time travel takes place. This scientifically verifiable   and   mathematically   and   quantum   physically provable fact alone makes it worthwhile to deal in detail with the topic of quantum physics and quantum healing.

In this technique it is imperative that the healer maintains the state of pure consciousness. Should he leave the pure consciousness due to a concentration disorder or an external disturbing factor, the process is stopped. Furthermore, this is the only technique of quantum healing where the patient can actually feel something like discomfort, in some cases even a feeling of fear. As already explained, this is the preferred method for solving emotional problems. Some of these problems can be traced back to considerable mental blockages. In some cases the cause can even be found in traumas that the patient experienced in his childhood. But if you have the courage to engage in this fascinating technique, you will find that the dissolving and processing of your inner emotional blockages can give you a feeling of life and a positive attitude towards yourself and your fellow human beings, as they were actually able to experience it for the last time as a carefree child in some cases.

The 5 A quantum therapy

With the Timeline method we have chosen the physical level of our macro-universe as our starting point, in the form that we have expanded the pure consciousness of quantum healing by the factor of *time.* With the 5 A Quantum Therapy, which is often casually called 5 A by experienced quantum healers, we are now moving another step towards our physical reality, of course without neglecting the quantum and information level and the pure consciousness of quantum healing.

The 5 A Quantum Therapy combines elements of quantum healing, i.e. pure consciousness, with the physical component already known from the two-point method, i.e. physical touch. What is new in this method, however, is that a mental component is added to this technique.

In principle, 5 A quantum therapy is about the patient thinking consciously, i.e. letting   himself be guided by the *intention of* healing already known from the two-point method. This is essentially no different from the goal that orthodox medical practitioners strive for in e.g. talk therapy, psychotherapy or, to a lesser extent, behavioral therapy. This represents the already mentioned even deeper anchoring of the 5 A quantum therapy on the physical level of our existence. But in the end it is again pure consciousness with which we gain access to the quantum level and the information level of our multi-layered physical and mental existence.

The five steps that lead to awareness and finally to an intention to heal in 5 A Quantum Therapy are the following:

1. Notes
2. Accept
3. Align
4. Acting
5. Staying on the ball

Special attention must be paid to the last point, staying on the ball. Because, in contrast to many other techniques from quantum healing, it is not possible with 5 A quantum healing to achieve quick and lasting success with only one single session. Instead, the patient must become aware of these five points again and again in order to permanently align his mental processes with the data of his perfect state of health stored on the information level and to ensure a slow and gradual transfer of the data associated with the state of *health* into his matrix. This continuous awareness is accompanied by the physical contact of the body, as known from the two-point method, whereby this technique should attempt to touch those points of the body where the problem has manifested itself. In this way, the matrix on the quantum level is carefully prepared for data transfer from the information level and the autonomic nervous system is also stimulated to ensure a fluid flow of the process.

You may now ask yourself why you should engage in a long-term quantum therapeutic treatment when you can achieve immediate success with another technique. Of course you are absolutely right. But please remember that other techniques, such as the sudden overwriting or resetting of the matrix, can lead to dizzy spells or even to fluctuations of the body, because, even if completely harmless, which should be emphasized again at this point, the sudden rearrangement of the physical energy matrix on the quantum level represents a radical, perhaps even traumatic process. Likewise, other techniques used to solve emotional problems can cause discomfort or, in extreme cases, even short-term anxiety attacks. These completely harmless, but nevertheless present side effects may in some cases prevent the patient, or people who are already interested in quantum healing, from using these techniques. The 5 A quantum therapy offers an alternative to these fast-acting techniques, with which the patient can produce exactly the same effect distributed over a longer period of time and therefore much more gently.

The hypnosis quantum healing after Dolores Cannon

Hypnosis quantum healing is probably the most powerful technique that exists in this alternative healing method. If all other techniques have reached their limits, then hypnosis quantum healing will enable you to achieve a breakthrough in solving your physical or mental problems, or even your stressful life circumstances with almost guaranteed certainty.

Hypnosis Quantum Healing combines the well-known basic elements of quantum healing with the hypnosis technique known as regressive hypnosis and used by many orthodox medical psychotherapists. This technique was developed by the American Dolores Cannon, who has not only invested almost 45 years of her life in the research, application and further development of regressive hypnosis, but has also achieved worldwide recognition and recognition as an author on this topic. So you can see that this technique of merging orthodox medicine and quantum healing is also preceded by recognition by physicians, psychologists and healers who are recognized and renowned in the field of orthodox medicine.

In contrast to all other techniques of quantum healing, hypnosis quantum healing is an exclusive external treatment. The involvement of an experienced hypnotist who is familiar with the basic principle of quantum healing, at least in its approaches, cannot be dispensed with in this treatment method. As explained in a previous chapter, there are also other techniques of quantum healing where the involvement of a third person is advisable, sometimes even indispensable. But in these cases it is always a matter of cooperation between healer and patient, i.e. the patient is also involved in the healing process in all these cases. Hypnotic quantum healing, on the other hand, is the only technique of quantum healing where a clear distinction is made between healer and patient. The patient is therefore passive, the healing is done exclusively by the healer, in this case the hypnotist.

The hypnosis quantum healing usually extends over three to four appointments. The duration of the individual appointments can vary greatly. Usually a time window of three to five hours is scheduled. In the first session the objective is defined concretely. Here it cannot be avoided that the patient gives the hypnotist, who is usually unknown to him, a leap of faith and is willing to tell him about his physical, emotional or personal problems in the form of money worries or relationship problems. After in the first session the goals, i.e. the *intention* already known from other techniques, have been clearly outlined, the patient is put into a deep trance in the second session. The hypnotist gains access to the patient's subconscious, where he can, through careful suggestion, bring about the state of pure consciousness necessary for quantum healing, without any active intervention by the patient.

After in the second session the state of pure consciousness, and thus the contact to the quantum and information level, which is indispensable for quantum healing, has been established, the hypnotist can in the third and fourth session, through further suggestions and specific questions, which should uncover problems in the patient's subconscious, gain access to the ideal state of the patient on the information level and make a new adjustment of the matrix. Since the patient is in a deep, relaxing trance, side effects are not to be expected even in case of a jerky data exchange between the information level and the patient's matrix.

Of course it should be mentioned that hypnosis quantum healing is not only probably the most effective but also the most content-intensive technique of quantum healing. Three or four appointments of three to five hours each with a hypnotist or a psychotherapist trained in hypnosis can be a financial investment for some people, which should be thought through first. But under no circumstances, in order to save money, should you try to perform this technique on yourself or in cooperation with a trusted person who is not trained in the use of medical hypnosis. First try the other techniques described in this book, which are in most cases free of charge. Only when your individual problem proves to be so deep-seated that the normal and in most cases successful free techniques can no longer provide any relief, should you think about resorting to the paid help of a professional quantum physician.

Instructions for the practical and regular implementation of quantum healing

The practical application of quantum healing

You have now learned a lot about the history, the scientific background and finally about the different techniques and methods of quantum healing. But perhaps you have not yet tried quantum healing because, whatever is a good and systematic approach, you will want to read this book in its entirety before dealing with this new and possibly very fascinating topic in practice. But perhaps you have not yet tried quantum healing because you have not yet been able to get a clear idea of how exactly you should proceed.

If the latter is the case, then I would like to remedy the situation here and provide you with a detailed step-by-step guide that will help you to overcome this first inhibition threshold, which is actually very common. And indeed, I would like to advise you to simply get involved right now. So read the following instructions once or twice until you have internalized them, and then put this book aside to take the first of many steps on the path to physical and mental health through quantum healing and the resulting reorganization of your matrix through contact with the information level.

1. Find a comfortable place in your apartment. This can be your sofa, a chair, or you can also lie down in your bed. The important thing is that you can relax. You might also provide a quiet musical background or create a pleasantly scented atmosphere with incense sticks or essential oils. It is best to switch off your cell phone. It is important that you

can relax in peace and quiet without the possibility of interference from external influences in the back of your mind.

2. Now place the finger of one of your hands on a part of your body that causes you discomfort. If you cannot define this particular area exactly, simply let your feelings guide you. There is no right or wrong, only good, better and best. If you are tormented by mental or psychological problems, you can choose your heart or forehead as a starting point. For relationship problems or money worries the stomach is recommended, because these kinds of problems and people often hit the stomach.

3. Next, either place the finger of your other hand or the entire palm of your hand on another part of your body. It does not matter which place you choose. You will subconsciously follow the energy streams of your matrix and instinctively find the right place, or more precisely, it is physically impossible to find the wrong place. Some kind of trust or feeling is not necessary at all. You follow physical laws of nature, not your feeling.

4. Now take on the role of the observer as described in the previous chapter. Relax, breathe calmly and deeply. You can let your thoughts drift aimlessly. You do not have to suppress your emotions or even physical pain. Just keep breathing calmly and steadily, observe your breathing, your body, your thoughts and feelings, and you will quickly find your way into the described state of pure consciousness.

5. Now try to maintain this state of pure consciousness as long as you can. One more step, one more activity is not necessary. It is the state of pure consciousness that leads to a connection with the information level and the subsequent healing without your further action. Just enjoy this state as long as it lasts.

Normally, you will experience a significant improvement in your state of health the first time. However, it can happen that the hoped-for effect does not occur with first-time users because, for example, disturbing thoughts or general doubts about the effectiveness of quantum healing as a scientifically justifiable and explainable method can disturb the state of pure consciousness and prevent contact with the information level. It is also possible that there are deeper-seated blockages whose existence you are not even aware of and which, as the cause of your individual problem, must first be removed before healing can take place on the symptomatic level.

As a rule, the soothing and healing effect of quantum healing increases with each time you practice it. As with everything in life, practice makes perfect. However, if after three or at the latest four sessions you do not at least show first clearly visible progress, it is possible that a deeper-seated blockage is indeed preventing you from alleviating your problems on the symptomatic level. In this case you should seek the advice of an experienced quantum healer or alternative practitioner to analyze the problem on a deeper level.

Quantum healing in everyday life in relation to self-healing

Maybe all this may seem very complicated to you. And the preparations I recommended in the previous chapter, turning off your cell phone, creating a relaxed atmosphere, may give you the impression that quantum healing can only be practiced as an experience removed from your everyday life. In fact, it is exactly the other way around. The five-step instruction presented here explicitly referred to newcomers to this subject. For an experienced quantum healer, or someone who has gained a bit of routine in the course of perhaps four or five sessions, quantum healing can be practiced practically at any time and place.

It is absolutely possible that you put yourself in a state of pure consciousness while sitting in the morning on the suburban train and going to work, or standing in the supermarket queue, or getting your hair cut at the hairdresser. Of course, the Quantum Entrainment technique is the method of your choice here, because it would look a bit strange if you started fumbling around in the supermarket queue. But remember, the state of pure consciousness in the form of Quantum Entrainment is based on unintentional observation. So when you stand in the supermarket queue, you are observing the people standing around you without intention or judgment. If you are sitting in the suburban train and you are being bombarded by noisy loudspeaker announcements, put yourself in the role of the uninvolved, value-free observer. With a little practice, you can put yourself in the state of pure consciousness in any situation, even if it is only for a few healing seconds. This ability will enable you to relax stressful situations by concentrating for only seconds and by having contact with the information level for only a microsecond. In fact, you will find that this approach will not only affect you, but also the situation itself and all the people connected to this situation. Make it a habit to immerse yourself in the state of pure consciousness several times a day for very short periods of time and you will draw behind you a wake of relaxation, calmness and healing that is visible and perceptible to everyone.

Quantum healing in everyday life in relation to external healing

In the course of this book so far, you have learned that 1. there are various techniques for successfully applying the method of quantum healing that can be performed alone or in collaboration with others, and that 2. some of the scientifically explainable physical and quantum physical laws of nature on which quantum healing is based can be traced back to Thomas Young's double-slit experiment from 1902. Both the knowledge gained from this experiment and from all the findings about quantum physics in theoretical speculations and practical experiments since then clearly point to one of the most important laws of nature that exist at the quantum level. In the course of this book, this important finding has not been discussed in detail, or even emphasized in any noteworthy way, although this law at the quantum level is at least as important as the factors of space, time and gravity in our macro-universe. The reason why this factor has been deliberately withheld from you, and why it should only be dealt with on the surface now, is simply that a closer look would simply go beyond the scope of this book. In comparison: the existence of the natural law of gravity alone fills entire scientific libraries. In this book, however, the focus will be on quantum healing and its explanation by quantum physics, and not on quantum physics itself. Therefore, I ask for your understanding that the physical and quantum physical laws of nature underlying the following technique of quantum healing can only be partially illustrated and explained here.

This double-slit experiment has led to the compelling conclusion not only that the motion of particles reacts to the observation of a conscious mind and even behaves according to the expectations of this conscious observer, but also that the motion of particles is interdependent on each other, regardless of their location in space and time. This means that particles, as well as bodies made up of particles, interact with each other at both the macroscopic and quantum levels, regardless of the distance between them. If you have ever studied the alternative healing method of Reiki, this information will be nothing new for you. In Reiki, it is completely normal that patients can be healed by specially trained healers over long distances, which is ultimately due to the interaction of particles on the quantum level.

Very briefly: You can not only heal yourself by putting yourself in the state of pure consciousness, but you can also heal other people, without physical touch, by putting yourself in the state of pure consciousness and then focusing on said people. Or you can heal each other with another person who also masters the technique of Quantum Healing by using pure consciousness. Each of the two people involved puts himself in the state of pure consciousness and concentrates on the other person, whereby, as has already been described elsewhere, the healing energy does not add up, but rather increases. In this way, you can achieve a level of healing and well-being that you would never experience with pure self-healing.

According to the experiences from the double-slit experiment and the technique of healing with Reiki, which was successfully used in the years before the mentioned experiment, it is also not necessary for you to be in the same room as your partner during the mutual healing through quantum physical processes. In theory, it does not even matter whether you are on the same planet or in the same galaxy. The interaction of particles, which has been proven by the double-slit experiment and various subsequent scientific experiments, works universally, i.e. completely independent of the space existing between the particles.

Make use of this effect! You just have five minutes? Call a friend who also practices quantum healing and unite for a few beautiful moments in pure consciousness. Or arrange with your partner for a fixed time, exact to the minute. Maybe even when you are sitting at work. The anticipation of the moment of shared pure consciousness will give a whole new quality to your monotonous or stressful workplace, and the moment of shared pure consciousness will finally bring a relaxed smile to your lips and let your stressed or bored colleagues ask themselves once again why you are always in such a good mood.

Advanced external healing using quantum physical knowledge and methods

Quantum healing in animals

If you apply Quantum Healing to yourself or to another person, or if you let another person apply it to you, then two adult people interact with each other who have made a conscious decision to engage in this scientifically based and proven form of alternative healing. After all, this conscious decision is also one of the elementary factors that are necessary for the pure consciousness needed for a quantum healing and the subsequent or associated contact with the information level. But what if the person or the being to be healed is not capable of this conscious decision?

In this chapter we will now look at how we apply quantum healing to our loved ones. Please take it as a somewhat cheeky joke that I give animals priority over children. My wife knows what I mean. I am sure that you too know these little jokes from your current or former relationship, which only you and your partner can understand.

But enough of digressions. Let's get to the actual topic, namely how you can apply quantum healing to animals such as dogs, cats, hamsters, etc., but also to e.g. horses or cows. There are no limits here. Quantum healing affects all living beings that are formed from moving particles and whose original blueprint is stored as a possibility state on the information level of reality.

The problem with the treatment of animals with quantum healing is obviously that the animal, at least in the first moment, does not know what you are actually doing. Once the process of quantum healing has begun, you will very quickly realize that the animal you are treating will try in its own unique way to support you in the treatment you are performing. This is because animals, even better than humans, instinctively sense when something is good for them. Moreover, and this is one of the advantages of treating animals, but also of treating children, animals do not have as many hectic and disturbing thoughts as adults, which makes it easier for them to engage in the pure consciousness necessary for quantum healing treatment.

The basic prerequisite for starting treatment with your pet is relaxation. For example, if it is a dog or cat that you want to treat, you can bring your pet into a relaxed state by stroking it and by using calming words. It is possible that at this point the pet will instinctively register what your intention is and will therefore be able to engage in the process with confidence.

Now, as with the two-point method, first place a finger somewhere on the body of your pet and concentrate. If you can locate the exact spot where a physical problem exists, this is advantageous. Otherwise, simply let your gut feeling guide you. Your instinct will not deceive you.

Now that you have reached the state of pure consciousness, as described in a previous chapter, place the finger of your other hand anywhere on the body of the animal, whereby, just like the treatment of people with quantum healing, it does not matter where you place the second hand or finger. In contrast to the first finger, the second finger does not have a healing but a deductive function, which I will not go into at this point, however, in order not to unnecessarily complicate the complexity of this topic and its connection to quantum physical laws.

Let the energy flow and relax. Your pet will feel and reflect your relaxation, which will have a positive effect on the treatment. When your pet finally has enough, it will let you know. Under no circumstances should you prevent an animal that wants to stop the treatment, for example by trying to stand up. The relationship of trust between your animal and you is of fundamental importance, and not only in relation to a treatment with quantum healing. Let your animal have its way. Trust that it will instinctively sense and tell you through its behavior when the current process of treatment is complete, and it will give you its fullest trust in subsequent treatments and make the process an experience that will lead to an even deeper and more lasting bond between you and your little companions.

Quantum healing in children

Since, as has already been described many times, quantum healing is not only used to correct physical ailments, but also serves as an excellent tool to decelerate and calm down our often hectic everyday or working life, it is also an alternative healing method for the prevention of psychological and psychosomatic complaints caused by stress and excessive demands on the smallest and weakest members of our society. Often our children are exposed to pressure to perform from kindergarten onwards, e.g. through courses designed to prepare them for elementary school. Later on, various appointments are made, since nowadays a child should not only be active in a sports club and be practiced in the use of at least one instrument, but also have to spend part of his or her free time, which is actually reserved for the child, in learning groups or professional tutoring. Later, when the child reaches adolescent maturity, the social pressure of modern communication media such as Facebook and WhatsApp, with its constant accessibility and social tension, does the rest. It is not for nothing that nowadays you have to wait up to two years for a free place at a child and youth psychologist. And while the average age of patients in therapy facilities specializing in burnout syndrome was 45 to 48 years 20 years ago, it has now dropped to mid-20s.

As an all-encompassing healing method, which not only corrects physical and psychological complaints that have already broken out, but also has an effect on disturbances in the way people live their lives, quantum healing is excellently suited to alleviating problematic constellations and performance pressure situations, especially in children and young people, before these can materialize on the psychological or physical level. And perhaps it is not even necessary to reduce the pressure to perform as the cause of possible secondary diseases . Sometimes it may be sufficient to give the child or adolescent the mental and emotional stability he or she needs to cope with the stressful everyday life at school and in his or her free time by means of regular quantum therapeutic applications, without losing sight of the core element, the most urgent main task, namely *being* the *child.*

The application of Quantum Healing is relatively simple for young people, because after the process has been explained to them, they can make a conscious decision to accept and accept this healing method internally, or they can simply learn it themselves. For children and toddlers, however, whose understanding cannot, for understandable reasons, grasp the basic structures of an alternative healing method based on quantum physical laws, a different approach is necessary.

Since Quantum Healing should be used in a state of relaxation, you can engage in a relaxing activity with your child as a preparation. Play his favorite game with him, run a radio play or read a book to him. Create a relaxing atmosphere in which your child can engage in something new and open himself completely to the energies of pure consciousness.

The application itself shall not be replayed here. Simply use one of the methods described in detail above, which you have learned in the meantime and perhaps already tried out on yourself or with a partner. The only thing that remains to be mentioned is that quantum healing, due to its mode of action, is virtually predestined for treatment in children, because it allows the child's mind, free of prejudices as it is, to adjust much more quickly to the energies of pure consciousness and the associated contact with the quantum and information level. In addition, the child's matrix is of course even closer to the original data stored on the information level, because the child has not yet had as much time as adults to deviate from its original blueprint due to its age.

Quantum healing in plants

Perhaps you have bought this book to correct physical or mental problems with a novel alternative healing method based on scientific facts. In short: Maybe you are ill. And what do you do when you are ill? You go to the doctor. This is a procedure you are used to. Since early childhood, the image has been implanted in your consciousness that an illness entails a visit to a doctor, who in many cases is dressed in a white coat. And since this image has indeed burned itself very deeply into your conscious and subconscious mind, experience shows that the subject of quantum healing in plants leads to frowning, because it unconsciously creates the thoroughly humorous image in the back of your head of how you sit in the consultation room with a flower pot in your hand.

Say goodbye to this image and realize that a plant is not only a biological living being with a metabolic system and a vegetative nervous system, but also an object consisting of moving particles, whose basic information is stored in different possible levels on the information level and is realized via the quantum level. Of course you can use quantum healing for your plants! And since a plant does not have a consciousness and thought processes in the kind of higher developed life forms like us humans, even a disturbance of the healing process by distracting thoughts or prejudices is completely impossible. And this is exactly the reason why quantum healing in plants not only works, but actually works *excellently.*

To subject a plant to the process of quantum healing, you basically have two options. In a combination of

Quantum Entrainment and external healing as described above, you can bring the plant into contact with the information level by focusing on pure consciousness and projecting this consciousness onto the plant body. Or you can use the two-point method. In this case, proceed as described above. If, as is possibly the case with the treatment of animals, the cause of the problem cannot be clearly localized on the plant body, you can be guided by your instinct and your feeling. Remember that the plant is an object composed of moving particles, and your body is also an object composed of moving particles. And these parts interact with each other. There is really no possibility that you do anything wrong or, if you rely on your feeling, you miss the cause manifesting on the physical plane with your fingers or hands.

Quantum healing for unconscious persons

If quantum healing works even with plants that are incapable of consciousness, then it can of course also be applied to people who, due to their state of health, are not able to make a conscious decision and consciously participate in the healing process. Be it a person who is not able to understand and consciously support the process of quantum healing due to e.g. a mental limitation, or a person who is not conscious due to his current state of health either temporarily and temporarily or even long-term. In extreme cases, this would be, for example, a person who is in a coma.

In no case do I want to make false promises at this point. Quantum healing, as powerful as it may be as a tool in the repertoire of alternative healing methods, also has its limits. The probability that you will succeed in bringing a comatose patient back into the world of conscious life and experience is very small. But an improvement in the general health of said patients is quite achievable and has been documented several times. And indeed, it does occasionally happen that even comatose patients, even *without* quantum healing or other alternative healing methods, have regained consciousness. As I said, under no circumstances should false promises be made at this point. But possibly, and I emphasize *possibly,* the treatment of a person close to you who is in a coma may tip the scales in your favor.

Quantum physics and the information level as explanatory model for further alternative healing methods

Healing by laying on of hands, also known as Reiki

If this book is not your first entry into the fascinating world of alternative healing methods, which have been used since time immemorial and exist in innumerable variations, but if you have already dealt with other alternative healing methods in theory or perhaps also in many years of applied practice, then you have certainly noticed the parallels between the method of healing by laying on of hands called **Reiki** and certain techniques of quantum healing. However, at this point I must at least slightly curb your enthusiasm. There are clear parallels, this cannot be denied, but there are also differences.

The classical application of Reiki consists of a healer laying his hands on the patient. In this process, certain areas of the body are chosen, e.g., as in quantum healing, a place where pain or other obvious problems manifest themselves in the matrix on the physical level, or, in order to bring about an improvement in the general condition, certain energetically highly effective zones of the body are chosen to cover as large an area as possible and thus strengthen the healing effect. The chakras, the seven energy centers of the body, which you have probably heard of before, are very popular.

And although nothing exists in our physical world that does not exist on the quantum level or is not stored on the information level, this particular form of healing has very little to do with the basic physical principles of quantum healing. To illustrate this, the most elementary differences will be listed here.

1. The healer acts only as a channel for the healing energies during healing by laying on of hands as well as with other techniques used in Reiki, which will be explained in more detail in a moment. These energies are present all around us. They are always at work and to a certain extent even responsible for the self-healing powers of our bodies. A person who practices Reiki as a healer is only trained to consciously tap into these already existing healing powers, to guide them through his body and to transfer them through his hands in concentrated form into the body of another person. It is not necessary to be immersed in pure consciousness for this purpose. Of course the effect can be intensified by concentration on the part of the healer. But in the end, it is not about establishing contact with the information level, but only to redirect and concentrate the energy already flowing around us.

2. When another person is treated by a quantum healer during quantum healing, then automatically a healing effect always takes place with the healer himself. This is, so to speak, an unavoidable side-effect of putting oneself in the state of pure consciousness. In Reiki, however, the healer is only a channel. The energies flow like water through a pipe through his body. The healing effect, however, occurs only at the end of this imaginary pipe, as at the exit points at the hands, where they then

flow into the body of another person and develop the healing effect.

3. Since the healer only acts as a channel in Reiki, it is not possible for him to heal himself. This would be like a pipe trying to let the water flow back into itself. This is physically as well as quantum physically completely impossible. Therefore, even the strongest and most experienced healer who uses the method of Reiki is dependent on the help of another healer in case of illness.

4. As a direct consequence of point three, in contrast to quantum healing, it is of course also not possible to practice Reiki alone. At least two people must always be involved in the healing process. It is also not possible for one healer in Reiki to heal two or more people. However, what is feasible and is often done is that one person is treated by several healers at the same time, that is, several healers lay their hands on the body of the person to be healed. Here, however, the united healing energy is not potentiated like in the union of several pure states of consciousness with each other, but only added up. Nevertheless, according to statements by people who have undergone this kind of intensive treatment, the resulting process has been overwhelming and the healing process has been above expectation.

5. Since this healing energy is an actual physical energy that can be made visible with physical measuring instruments such as a magnetometer, at least in a very small form, no intervention by the patient is necessary. In quantum healing, the process that is to lead to a connection to the information level can be disturbed or even completely interrupted by disturbing thoughts or prejudices against this type of treatment. Reiki has the advantage over quantum healing that, just like a drug prescribed by a doctor, it always works, even if the patient does not want to believe it.

6. And finally, as already described, the healing energy of Reiki is an energy that has its origin in our physical macro-universe. Of course this energy also exists on the quantum level and is also stored as an unchangeable data set on the information level. But the functional principle of Reiki is simply completely different from quantum healing. There is no access to the information level with the goal of changing the patient's state of potentiality by overwriting the disturbed matrix with a new data set.

But if you are already involved with Reiki or even already practising this alternative healing method, i.e. if you know *that* Reiki works, and if you know *how* Reiki works because you have taken a course in it, and you are now hoping to get the answer from this book as to why it works, then I don't have to disappoint you. Because in addition to healing through Reiki by laying on of hands, there is also the possibility to heal people through remote Reiki. And here the quantum mechanical laws really take effect, as you already know from the functioning of quantum healing over long distances.

That of healing through Reiki over long distances, the healer focuses on the patient. But instead of placing his hands directly on the patient's body, the healer performs a series of specific gestures to channel the energy. It has already been described elsewhere that due to quantum mechanical laws all particles interact with each other, regardless of the distance between them. This is not only true for moving physical particles, but also for energy fields or energy waves. As an example: Gravitational fields influence each other, and they also influence the physical particles in their sphere of influence. And since there is also an interaction between energies and particles, it is no problem for the healer to transfer the physical healing energy, which he absorbs in our macro-universe at his respective location, over any distance via the quantum level to his patient.

Healing through homeopathy in the form of energetic information

In the previous chapter it was explained that although the energy in Reiki healing originates in our physical universe, quantum physical laws are applied when using this alternative healing method in the form of distance Reiki. It is therefore quite possible that a combination of factors between the macro-universe and the quantum universe offers the possibility of a successful healing and that quantum physical laws are applied to elements which under normal circumstances can be assigned to the normal physical laws of our macro-universe.

Homeopathy even goes one step further in this respect. In homeopathy, a physical element, i.e. a materially available, tangible and measurable substance consisting of molecules, is transferred in its mode of action not only to the quantum level, but even to the information level.

The basic principle of homeopathy will most likely be familiar to you. A very brief summary: In homeopathy, a physical agent, practically a medicine, is mixed with a carrier liquid such as water. Through the interaction of the molecular particles, an exchange between the potent preparation and the water takes place on a molecular basis. The liquid is then further diluted, whereby, apparently in defiance of common sense, the fewer particles of the original preparation are contained in the liquid, the more the effectiveness of the homeopathic remedy increases. This dilution can go so far that the remedy no longer contains molecules of the original preparation, but only the information of this preparation, which was previously exchanged on a molecular basis between the preparation and the water molecules.

You can probably see where this is heading. The information for healing has been stored on the physical plane in the water molecules through the interaction of moving particles. Furthermore, the information for the patient's state of health is stored on the information level in the form of the possibility state of *being healthy.* To use a false picture that explains the process well, imagine that the information level is vibrating at a certain frequency. And imagine that the preparation physically present in our macro-universe would also vibrate at a certain, but completely different frequency. By mixing and diluting the preparation, the homeopathic remedy is gradually brought closer and closer to its pure healing information. Little by little, the frequency of the homeopathic remedy is brought closer and closer to the frequency of the information level until both finally oscillate at exactly the same frequency.

At this point one could argue about whether here a part of the information level is transferred to the physical level, or whether a part of the physical level is transferred to the information level, or whether it doesn't matter at all, since according to the known quantum physical laws it is also quite possible that both are true at the same time. Ultimately it does not matter and does not change the fact that due to this extremely close connection between the physical level and the information level, homeopathy is probably one of the most effective remedies in the repertoire of alternative healing methods.

Healing through visualization as a subform of pure conscious-ness

If homeopathy can be considered one of *the* most powerful tools in the repertoire of alternative healing methods, then healing through visualization is probably *the* most powerful tool. After all, it is to a considerable extent our thoughts and the images rooted in our consciousness and subconscious that determine our being and, due to a positive or negative influence, have an influence on our state of health to an extent that should not be underestimated.

The visualization as alternative healing method, in appropriate professional circles from as **itself healthy thinking** describes, is not only extremely effective, but in their application also most easily feasible. In very simplified terms, it is simply a matter of the patient imagining a certain image of how a disease from which he or she is suffering could be cured, and repeatedly visualizing this image in his or her mind's eye, for so long and so often and so intensively, until this imaginary image finally becomes a physical reality.

The effectiveness of healing through visualization as well as the agreement to quantum healing is obvious. If the patient in quantum healing strives for the state of **pure consciousness in** order to gain access to the information level on a very general level, then in healing through visualization the patient repeatedly **recalls** a very specific image in order to gain access to a small and very specific area of the information level. This is the specific area where the information for the realization of the image is stored.

An even clearer correspondence between quantum healing and healing through visualization becomes apparent when comparing healing through visualization with the two-point method in quantum healing, because in both techniques the conscious intention to heal brings about success.

In a broader perspective, healing through visualization can also be associated with the phenomenon of the placebo effect, or with what is commonly known as positive thinking. Psychologists or coaches working with motivating techniques also make use of this effect. But no matter how you twist and turn it, it is always the awareness that with an intention, which can be positive or negative, obvious or hidden, accesses the information level of our reality and thus transfers via the quantum level as a catalyst the state of possibility we desire, or unfortunately sometimes undesired, to the physical level of our macro-universe.

The best medicine is the one you do not need

How to stay healthy so you don't have to use quantum healing or any other alternative healing method

It may have been different motivations that led you to buy this book. Perhaps you are ill and looking for a healing method as an alternative to the therapy suggested by your doctor, or as a support for one. Perhaps you are active in the field of alternative healing methods and would like to receive further training. Or maybe it was just scientific interest that led you to get involved with this fascinating topic. But regardless of your motivation and personal life situation, there is one thing that simply remains the same: The best medicine, the best healing method is always the one you don't need. The best thing is not to get sick in the first place.

But you can't choose that, you might think now. And in most cases you are absolutely right. A genetic predisposition to diabetes or cancer. An accident in car traffic or cycling through no fault of your own. The inevitable cold or flu you catch at work or in the supermarket in winter. All this is part of our lives and in most cases it is unavoidable.

But does diabetes or cancer necessarily have to be severe or even fatal? How long does it take to recover from the accident or sports injury? And why do some people get the flu and others don't, even though they were exposed to the same virus at the same time and place?

So you see, it is not quite that simple. And there are in fact a lot of things you can do to either prevent a disease in the first place, or at least mitigate its course. For this reason, I would like to conclude this book with a few tips and tricks on how you can use a healthy lifestyle to prevent the possibility of **being ill, which you have** stored on the information level but which you do not want to have, from becoming a quantum physical possibility and finally a physical reality.

Stay relaxed and avoid stress

In many cases, stress and hectic are the triggers for psychological and psychosomatic illnesses and are often realized on the physical level in the form of stomach ailments or chronic tension. In order to avoid this, you should make sure that you relax regularly and not only give your body some rest, but also let your soul dangle.

Here are a few tips on how to get through the day in a relaxed manner.

Tip number 1:
A positive start to the day is the beginning of a successful and relaxing day

A bad start to the day is one of the worst things that can happen to you. Stress is already pre-programmed, hectic and dissatisfaction is inevitable. Avoid being pressed for time in the morning. Plan your morning in such a way that you have enough time to devote to the tasks of your morning routine. Set your alarm clock to the appropriate time and give yourself a jolt when it rings. Get up and face the day with motivation and zest for life instead of turning around two, three or four times. This is the only way you will be able to complete your morning routine in the bathroom relaxed and without time pressure. Also plan enough time to allow yourself an extensive and healthy breakfast. Breakfast is the most important meal of the day. And even if it's just coffee for you, make sure you have enough time to enjoy this personally appropriate start to the day in peace and quiet.

Tip number 2:
Just put your feet up, let your soul dangle and your thoughts wander

Find a place where you feel comfortable. Maybe your sofa, a deck chair in the garden, if the weather allows it, or take a blanket and lie down in a meadow in nature. Take something to drink and maybe a book. Or just let your thoughts drift. Or consciously think of something beautiful, a positive memory, or an interesting dream you had. Just switch off, and the relaxation of your thoughts will also have an effect on your body. Do this regularly and very consciously, and you will notice over time that you carry these relaxing moments within you and build up a feeling towards them that can best be explained with the familiar image of the eye of the storm or the rock in the surf. And if you find yourself in a stressful situation once again, it will be the memory of and anticipation for these beautiful moments that will create a place of calm within you.

Tip number 3:
Relax with a long, pleasant bath

The classic relaxation bath, one of the most well-known and obvious tools in the repertoire of relaxation possibilities, not only helps to bring your soul to rest, but also has very concrete physical effects. The heat and the water have a calming effect on the body cells and also on the circulation and some of your organs. You can lie back in the tub and close your eyes, or, if you have the time and plan a longer bath, you can read a book. However, it is not advisable to use a cell phone in the bathtub, as the hectic world of the Internet and social media, as well as the inner mental tension caused by the use of mobile games, counteracts the idea of relaxation. You can also experiment with bath additives, or with essential oils. If you have the opportunity, then you should choose the evening as the time for a relaxing bath.

Tip number 4:
Deal with something that gives you pleasure

Everyone needs a hobby. Every person should have at least one thing in his life, which he only does because it gives him fun and pleasure. But in today's hectic and performance-driven world, the misconception that this hobby must involve some activity or process of creation has become commonplace. The activity in the sports club. The appointments at the music school to learn to play the guitar, and at some point find yourself in a small band. The pursuit of creative hobbies, such as painting or pottery, which are activities with visible results. Volunteering, hiking or weekly meetings with the English Speaking Group. And if these are the things that you enjoy, that you can relax in, then that's exactly what you should do. But some people have so much to do in their busy schedules that it's the very thing that causes the stress. So make yourself aware that this is really about something that you enjoy. And if it's the evening in front of the TV and the season marathon of your favorite TV series, or just lying on the sofa and listening to music, then you should treat yourself to just that, and without a guilty conscience, because you're not being productive and wasting your time.

Tip number 5:
Make sure you take regular exercise

Sufficient and regular exercise is not only one of the basic pillars for maintaining your health, but has been proven to reduce stress. But here again, you should relax and not perform. The adrenaline-pumping team sport, in which you give your all so that your team wins, has a natural invigorating and positive effect on your health on a purely physical level. The two-hour endurance run, with which you train for participation in a half-marathon, gives you a feeling of strength and success and releases happiness hormones. But this has little to do with relaxation and finding inner peace.

Get into your car, drive into the nature and take a walk through the forest. The sunlight falls in filtered strips through the treetops, a soft, warm breeze makes the branches rustle softly, birds chirp, small animals rustle in the undergrowth, the scent of grass and flowers penetrates your nose ... Surely the very idea of this picture will make you relax inside.

Or take a bicycle tour. Not to perform, but to look at the landscape. Choose a route through an area that appeals to you personally, perhaps through nature again. Combine the bike tour with a stop at a nice restaurant, a visit to an ice cream parlor or a visit to a castle or museum. Get exercise and do sports. But do it to relax, not to add another element to your stressful and hectic everyday life, which is characterized by performance and goal achievement.

Tip number 6:
Take time for your friends or your partner

We humans are social beings. Without social contacts to other people who are important to us, we cannot exist. Therefore, it is essential that you take enough time for your friends or your partner. For example, have a nice evening with your partner, just the two of you alone at home. Make sure that you are not disturbed. For example, turn off your cell phone, preferably after you have told your friends on your Facebook account that you do not want to be disturbed tonight, so that someone does not suddenly show up at the door uninvited. Or plan an evening with your friends, e.g. a visit to the cinema followed by a meal. Or maybe a barbecue afternoon in the garden. We humans do not live for ourselves. And we do not perform for ourselves. We are emotionally and socially linked to the people around us and depend on sharing joy and suffering. Share your stress with your friends and you will soon realize that a problem you have been brooding about all the time will quickly go up in smoke on united shoulders.

Tip number 7
Program your body's muscle memory for relaxation

Perhaps you have heard the term **muscle memory.** The muscles of your body have a memory. Certainly there are a lot of activities in your everyday life that you carry out again and again. And if you carry out an activity often enough, then at some point you no longer have to think about what you are doing, but your body moves almost by itself. A very good example of this is the activity on a computer. You have to get used to a new program in your private or professional life. In the beginning you concentrate on executing the recurring keyboard strokes and mouse clicks. But after a while it gets faster and faster, and at some point you don't think about it at all anymore because the sequence of the individual work steps has been imprinted in your muscle memory.

Take advantage of this and program your body and muscle memory to relax. Not much is needed at all. Just lean back for two minutes, take a few deep breaths and consciously relax the muscles of your body. Or when you are at home, just sit down on your sofa for two minutes in between and allow yourself a short break and a short relaxation. The important thing here is that you do this as often as possible, preferably once an hour and spread out over the whole day. Your body will get used to the relaxation and will then tend to relax rather than tense up even in stressful situations.

There is even another trick to it. Do these recurring relaxation exercises at fixed times, as far as you can. For example, if you work in the office, two minutes of relaxation every hour on the hour. This connects your muscle memory with your inner clock, which, by the way, works much more precisely than you might be aware of. Program the muscles of your body to relax at a certain, fixed time. And if you forget this, you will suddenly find that you are relaxing for no apparent reason, then look at the clock and realize that it is exactly the time that you have programmed into your muscles.

Exercise regularly and pay attention to your diet

You are what you are. To maintain your health, make sure you eat a balanced diet. Your body is dependent on a regular supply of vitamins, minerals and trace elements. Without this continuous supply, diseases due to deficiencies or consequences are possible. In addition, a lack of vitamins weakens the immune system and makes it more likely that you will fall ill from e.g. a virus or a bacterial effect that your body would normally have survived without symptoms. So make sure that you eat a healthy diet. In today's affluent times, it is no longer a problem to buy fresh fruit and vegetables at the supermarket. A few clicks of the mouse will also give you access to nutritional tables on the Internet or to a wide range of recipes.

You should also keep your fluid intake under observation. It is recommended to drink at least two liters of fluid per day. This not only prevents flaccidity and fatigue, but also allows your body to flush out accumulated toxins that have accumulated in your body, e.g. from chemically treated foods.

And last but not least, you should make sure you exercise regularly. That doesn't have to be the same for team sports or demanding competitive sports. As already mentioned in the previous chapter, a relaxing walk in the fresh air, perhaps even through nature, is perfectly sufficient and will also help you to reduce stress. But no matter if you go for a walk, to the gym or to competitive sports, you should do something, because we humans generally do not exercise enough nowadays and many illnesses are due to a long lasting lack of exercise.

With this we have already reached the end of this book. I thank you for reading and hope that I have succeeded in giving you an insight into the background of quantum healing as well as other alternative healing methods. If you have any further questions, suggestions or criticism, please do not hesitate to contact me at the email address thomas.drachentoeter@gmail.com. I am happy to answer questions of all kinds and am always open to criticism.

Finally, I would like to ask you to write me an honest review. If you liked this book, then a good review is welcome. If not, then a more differentiated and less good one. But I would like to ask you to be fair and actually evaluate the book, not the topic. If you couldn't find access to quantum healing with this book, then that's a pity, but I don't buy a book about make-up tips and then rate it badly because I personally as a man can't do anything with it. I have put a lot of effort into this book, and it would be a pity if it were to be stamped into the ground by a bad review just because someone has a bad day.

With this I say goodbye to you. Thank you again for reading, and perhaps we will meet again in another book of mine.

Thomas Drachentöter

Made in the USA
Monee, IL
12 February 2022